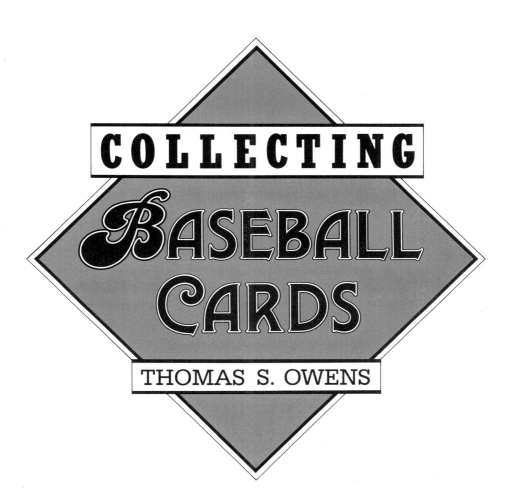

COLLECTING BASEBALL CARDS

THOMAS S. OWENS

The Millbrook Press
Brookfield, Connecticut

For Diana Helmer

Cards used on cover © and reproduced with permission of
Action Packed Cards, LBC Sports, Inc.; Mother's Cookies;
Pacific Trading Cards, Inc.

Photos and cards © and reproduced courtesy of The Topps Company, Inc.: pp. 10, 19, 26 (top right), 27, 34, 42 (right), 53, 55, 67;
Leaf-Donruss: pp. 11, 23, 26 (top left), 42 (left), 45, 61; author's
collection: pp. 13 (both), 14, 16, 20, 29, 38, 47, 63; Score: pp. 15,
25, 56; Classic: pp. 17, 41; Mother's Cookies: p. 18; Fleer: p. 26
(bottom); Ray Madeiros: pp. 31, 35, 36, 58; author's collection: p.
32; Upper Deck: pp. 52, 71.

Library of Congress Cataloging-in-Publication Data
Owens, Thomas S.
Collecting baseball cards / by Thomas S. Owens.
p.   cm.
Includes bibliographical references (p.   ) and index.
Summary: Provides practical advice on building a baseball card
collection, covering such topics as trading cards, preserving them,
and finding rookie cards, errors, and other specialties.
ISBN 1-56294-254-9 (LIB.)/ISBN 1-56294-713-3 (TR.)
1. Baseball cards—Collectors and collecting—Juvenile literature.
[1. Baseball cards—Collectors and collecting.]   I. Title.
GV875.3.O84   1993
796'.49796357'075—dc20   92-18166   CIP   AC

CONTENTS

COLLECTING
BASEBALL CARDS

CARDS, CARDS, CARDS

Here's a quick quiz: Why are more baseball cards available now than ever before?

Easy. Because there are more baseball card collectors out there than ever before. Baseball fans of all ages, everywhere, are collecting cards.

For proof, grab a telephone directory and turn to the Yellow Pages. Under the heading "Baseball Cards" or "Sports Cards," you'll likely find at least one listing. While you may be collecting cards for fun, many adults use the hobby as their careers, running hobby shops or buying and selling cards in other settings.

Imagine dozens, or even hundreds, of hobby shops under one roof. This is a collectors convention. These events take many forms, from a few card tables assembled in a church basement to the yearly National Sports Collec-

If you forget that Topps is the oldest card company around, just look at the 1991 set. The manufacturer bragged about its birthday on every card that year, using a special design.

tors Convention. At the "National," more than a hundred thousand collectors come together, looking for cardboard treasures during this four-day event.

Still not convinced? Go to the magazine rack at your nearest grocery or drug store. Start counting the number of publications written for people just like yourself—card collectors. Look closely and you should find at least a dozen titles of magazines. While most are monthly periodicals, one (*Sports Collectors Digest*) is issued every week.

Why are there so many magazines? Again, because there are so many collectors demanding more information about cards.

A statistical survey conducted for Action Packed Football Cards revealed some amazing numbers. This study estimated that between June 1990 and June 1991, $926 million was spent on baseball cards. Further, nearly 15 million collectors were in-

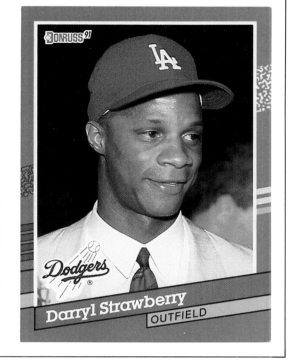

In 1991, Donruss began issuing its set in two series, making half the cards available at a time. Releasing the last half of the set at a later date gave the company time to include newer photos, such as Darryl Strawberry on the day he announced he was leaving the Mets and signing with the Dodgers.

volved with baseball cards, compared with 4 million for football cards, 3.1 million for basketball, and 1.6 million for hockey.

But is baseball card collecting still a hobby? Or with millions of people and dollars involved, is it a business?

Everyone debates that question. Some adults miss what they call "the good old days." Kids in the 1950s paid less than a nickel per pack for cards. No price guides existed, and collectors wanted only to complete sets.

Trades were easy to make, and many young people used cards as noisemakers clothespinned to the spokes of their bicycle wheels.

The bad part about the "good old days" was that collectors had trouble obtaining older cards. Some parents, thinking that the cards were worthless junk, threw them out. Today, some grown-ups moan that they could be rich if Mom or Dad hadn't trashed their collections!

In the 1960s and 1970s, too, baseball card collecting seemed simpler. Topps was the only company around, usually producing one 660-card set yearly. Now, collectors talk about the "big five"—Topps, Score, Donruss, Fleer, and Upper Deck—all major producers of baseball cards. Topps, makers of baseball card sets since 1951, distributed more than a billion cards in 1990.

Just how many different newly produced baseball cards are there to choose from each year? No one really knows. If you want to count only the cards from sets that are available nationally through hobby dealers and public outlets such as toy stores, the numbers start at about eight thousand different cards yearly. That's a modest count, too! Remember, that doesn't include card sets printed by individual teams, cards distributed in selected parts of the country, or other specialized sets sold only through dealers.

One way to keep up with the fast-moving world of baseball card collecting is through constant study. To build a collection that will be rewarding in the future, make sure you understand the hobby's past. If you understand hobby history, you'll get an excellent introduction to baseball's heritage. As the game has changed and grown, cards have documented the sport's evolution.

Baseball Card Beginnings

For more than a hundred years, baseball fans have loved baseball cards.

The first cards appeared in packages of tobacco back in 1887. Today, such an idea seems wild. Were tobacco companies trying to trick children into smoking by offering them baseball cards with every purchase?

Supposedly, the famed shortstop Honus Wagner thought so. The Pittsburgh Pirates star, known as "the Flying Dutchman," insisted that his card be removed from cigarette packages. No one knows which brand featured the Wagner card, because the set (issued from 1909 to 1911) featured advertising from sixteen different brands of cigarettes.

Nearly all those cards were destroyed to avoid Wagner's threat of legal action. Less than a hundred of the celebrated cards have survived. A near-mint Wagner card from the "T206" series would bring anywhere from $100,000 to $500,000.

While this version of the Wagner card story is exciting, some collectors believe another tale. The cigarette card producers were accused of not paying players for using their names and faces on cards. Wagner is considered the first player in history to insist on receiving part of the profits for being included on baseball cards.

"Collector issues" are cards sold only through hobby dealers, produced mainly for collectors. These sets were made in the 1970s by Iowa card dealers.

The tobacco card craze died out when World War I (1917–1918) filled the thoughts of Americans young and old. Meanwhile, candy companies had only mixed success issuing cards in paper panels, with several cards on one section. There was one exception. Remember the song "Take Me Out to the Ballgame," and the line that said "buy me some peanuts and Cracker Jacks"? That famous snack company issued sets in 1914 and 1915.

In the 1930s, gum companies discovered the idea of selling cards in packs. Goudey Gum, a Boston company, became the decade's biggest name in cards, offering sets from 1933 to 1941. But during the 1940s, cards weren't taken seriously, either by companies or the public. World War II seemed more important than baseball or baseball card collecting. Paper was scarce, and many cards were recycled for use in the war effort.

Bowman, not Topps, was the first

The Bob Addis card, measuring slightly longer than the standard size, is from the 1953 Bowman set. After 1955, Topps purchased the rival company. Topps revived the Bowman name, producing a standard-sized card in 1990.

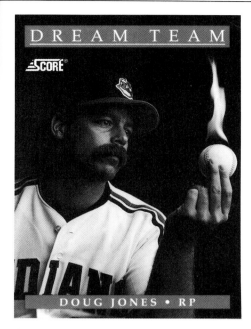

Since the 1950s, collectors have expected color baseball card photos. Score, in 1991, reversed that trend with an annual "Dream Team" subset. Celebrity photographer Annie Leibovitz helped create the artistic poses.

major company to create and market a set nationally after World War II. Beginning in 1948, Bowman issued yearly editions, growing to 240 cards in 1949. Topps became a rival in 1951. In 1955, Bowman issued its last set (with wood-grained borders meant to look like the cabinet of the newly popular color television sets). Topps purchased its competitor, issuing sets under the old company's name more than thirty years later.

Collectors remember 1981 as a milestone in hobby history. Topps, once considered the only kid on the block among card-makers, was challenged in court. Fleer and Donruss also wanted to make and distribute baseball cards. These competitors claimed that Topps had controlled the card business unfairly, making players promise not to appear on other sets.

The judges ruled against Topps in

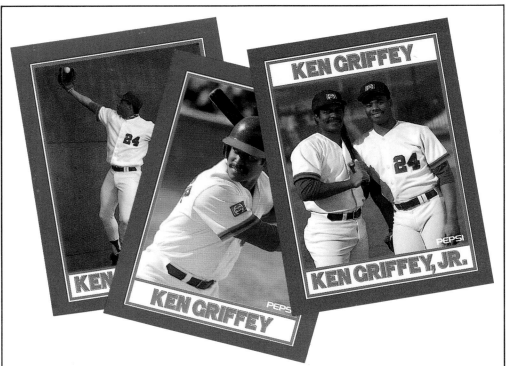

Regionals are sets issued only in certain geographic locations, often focusing on players or teams from that region. In 1991, an eight-card set honored the Griffeys, Seattle's father-and-son duo. Cards were offered in twelve-packs of Pepsi, or by buying drinks at Dairy Queen stores.

its quest to stop other companies from producing cards. However, Topps kept the right to be the only company to offer cards with "confectionery products," meaning gum or candy. Fleer and Donruss couldn't include gum in their card packs.

Ironically, that part of the legal decision became meaningless in 1991. Topps stopped including stiff slabs of pink chewing gum in packs. Why? The company heard collectors complaining about gum stains on cards from packs. Most of all, Topps realized that few fans liked to chew its famed creation.

Meanwhile, more card-makers joined the competition. Score began baseball card production in 1988, with Upper Deck following a year later.

Competing Card Companies

Companies big and small are fighting to become the top seller in a market overflowing with cards. This battle never stops.

Five different companies offer nationally issued sets of baseball cards. Topps, Donruss, Fleer, Score, and Upper Deck make many different sets each year, causing collectors to wonder how to buy (or even find) one of everything. Even if some lucky kids could afford such a collection, who has a closet big enough to hold it all?

Sports Collectors Digest reported that a total of 30,060 different baseball-related cards were issued in 1991, and that it would have taken at least $18,624.75 to obtain one of everything listed.

While *SCD* did the best job of documenting the flood of cards made for the year, even that list was far from complete. Cards were everywhere. Little-known "regional" sets, issued only in selected areas during a short time, have kept the hobby hopping.

For example, pitcher Sid Fernandez, a Hawaiian, was featured on special cards inserted in twelve-packs of soda pop in 1991. In Honolulu, these cards seemed easy to find. But collectors outside Hawaii may have never even heard about the issue.

This helps explain why many collectors limit their collecting to the baseball products of Topps, Donruss, Fleer, Score, and Upper Deck. These cards are favored because of their national availability. However, anyone who fails to consider the work of other companies might be missing out on some great hobby surprises.

Classic Games began making baseball cards in 1987. While the

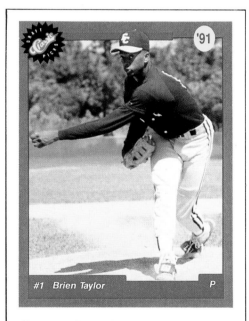

#1 Brien Taylor   P

Because Brien Taylor was signed to an exclusive contract with Classic Games to appear on this 1991 card, Upper Deck had to remove Taylor from its 1992 set at the last minute.

MOTHER'S COOKIES

A's and GIANTS

BASEBALL CARDS AND ½ PRICE TICKETS

½ PRICE A's
OAKLAND A's
PLAZA LEVEL TICKETS
REG. $8.00 SEATS—ONLY $4.00
COMPLIMENTS OF MOTHER'S COOKIES
FREE
TO THE FIRST 35,000 FANS
A's BASEBALL CARDS
SATURDAY, JULY 23, 1988 — 1:05 P.M.
AT THE OAKLAND COLISEUM
For details see coupons on 18 oz. bags of MOTHER'S COOKIES

BAY AREA CARD DAYS '88

½ PRICE
SAN FRANCISCO GIANTS
REG. $7.00 SEATS—ONLY $3.50
UPPER RESERVED SEAT TICKETS
COMPLIMENTS OF MOTHER'S COOKIES
FREE SAN FRANCISCO GIANTS
BASEBALL CARDS
TO THE FIRST 35,000 FANS—SATURDAY, JULY 30, 1988
1:05 PM — AT CANDLESTICK PARK
For details see coupons on 18 oz. bags of MOTHER'S COOKIES

AD SLICKS FOR YOUR CONVENIENCE

MOTHER'S COOKIES
18 oz. family size bags

chocolate chip
cookie parade
fudge'n chips
oatmeal raisin
cocadas

MOTHER'S COOKIES
18 oz. family size bags
chocolate chip   oatmeal raisin
cookie parade assortment
fudge'n chips
cocadas

½ PRICE
GIANTS and A's
RESERVED SEAT TICKETS
COMPLIMENTS OF
MOTHER'S COOKIES
SEE COUPON
EACH 18 OZ. BAG

A West Coast baking company, Mother's Cookies, began sponsoring team sets of cards in the 1980s. In 1988, Mark McGwire and Will Clark posed with their cards to promote an upcoming ballpark giveaway.

cards were designed first as quiz cards for a trivia board game, the Classic editions have developed large, dedicated groups of collecting fans. Each year, the sets contain amazing and sometimes bizarre photos. When Cubs slugger Andre Dawson was hit in the face with a pitch, the photo wound up in a Classic set. Another card showed Atlanta's David Justice posing in a judge's robe under the title "Justice Prevails."

Long before the major card companies expanded their sales to department and toy stores, Classic's board game was everywhere, along with its yearly sets featuring all new trivia questions. The company also became known for offering cards of high school and college players drafted by major-league teams.

Another little-known hobby treasure comes from Mother's Cookies, a bakery based in Oakland, California. Glossy, borderless team sets of colorful cards have been issued regionally since 1984. These cards are as close to actual photographs as a card collector can get. Smaller sets, distributed in cookie bag packages, devote four cards to a local hero, choosing names like Will Clark or Nolan Ryan.

Hobbyists haven't always supported the never-ending flow of sets. Donruss had little luck with postcard-size and "pop-up" sets. Fleer bombed with baseball stamps and a multitude of forty-four-card "star" sets. Each idea was retired when it failed to sell.

If the buyer has the last word in the

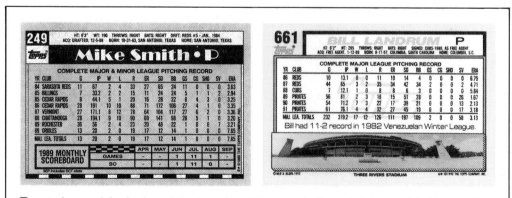

Topps changed the look and design of its 1992 baseball cards (shown right) from 1991 and past seasons. White card stock and color photos were firsts for the historic company.

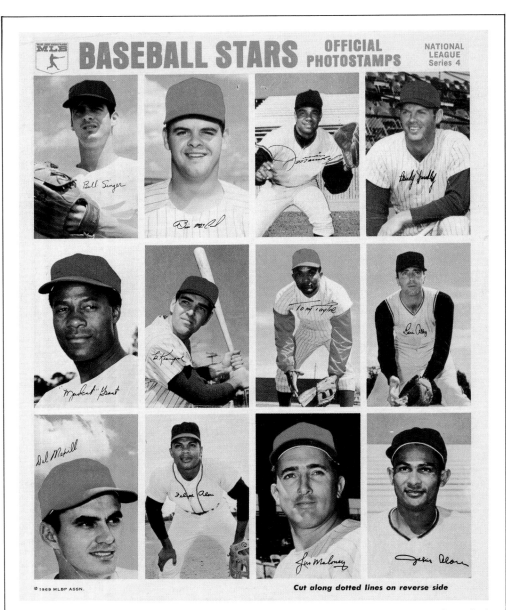

Producers of baseball cards sometimes remove or airbrush team names and symbols from photos. Why? Major League Baseball charges the card manufacturers for the right to use team logos, so it's cheaper to show players without team identifications.

card business, who has the first? Players and teams both want to control the kinds of cards made. The Major League Baseball Players Association and Major League Baseball (the office in charge of all teams) license sets. That's why only five major companies, instead of five hundred, print baseball cards.

The "NY" on Mets caps and the symbols on any team clothing are registered trademarks. Card-makers have to pay a fee to use any of those team markings on cards. Also, card-makers have to pay a royalty fee to players in exchange for using their faces. Every player appearing in sets can earn thousands of dollars each year from the cards you buy.

Teams and players like the money, but that's not the only reason they li-cense sets. Both groups work only with companies that let them approve the kinds of cards made.

This issue surfaced before the 1992 season began. Pro Set, famous for football and non-sport sets, planned to make "Flopps" cards, a sixty-six-card set of funny cartoons that would have parodied many stars. Rickey Henderson became "Stickey Henderson" and "Ryne Sunburn" was patterned after Chicago's Ryne Sandberg. But Pro Set said it gave up the idea in order to keep on good terms with the Major League Baseball Players Association. The group didn't like cards poking fun at individuals. Teams and players worry about their images, and they want cards that will promote the sport and themselves.

HOBBY STRATEGIES

One of the biggest mistakes anyone can make is to try to collect *every* baseball card produced each year. Remember, there is no hobby rulebook demanding that you collect only perfectly preserved sets of everything. Play by your own rules, designing the type of collection you'll enjoy the most.

Collecting on a Budget

Would you go to a restaurant and order all the foods listed on the menu? Of course not! Even if someone could pay for one of everything, no one could eat it all. But the many different baseball cards issued make choosing difficult, just like trying to pick out certain products at the grocery store. Adults know choosing is hard when they go to buy groceries, so they make shopping lists beforehand. Collectors should do the same. A "want list" is a simple list, spelling out what you want the most. Then, when you are visiting a card shop, other old and new sets won't be as tempting.

A want list will be easier to make after you decide on your hobby specialties. How about trying to obtain cards of all the players born in your state? Or starting a collection of only one team?

Some people like collecting cards from only one company. Other hobbyists might try to collect cards from the year they were born. Theme collections have become popular and affordable challenges for budget-minded baseball card fans.

Maybe you can make these decisions by elimination. If you decide the kinds of cards you *don't* like first, then your choices will get easier.

Every month, it seems, a new card set appears. You have to decide if each new issue belongs in your col-

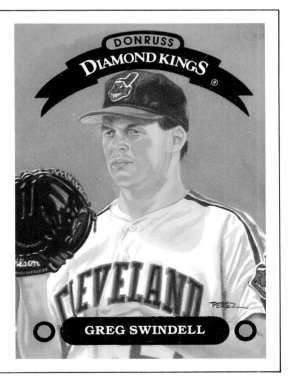

After ten years, Donruss stopped including "Diamond Kings" paintings by Dick Perez in its regular set. Instead, the cards were randomly inserted in foil packs, causing their supply to drop and their value to soar.

lection. You are like a manager choosing your starting lineup of players.

As you build your collection, you'll deal regularly with hobby dealers, people who sell cards. Most dealers are friendly, trustworthy adults who collect cards, too. Some may have other jobs and sell cards only part-time, at card shows, or by mail order. Others may be full-time dealers, running hobby shops or traveling around the country to sell at large conventions of collectors.

Newer collectors may fear they'll be cheated or tricked by all dealers, especially if they've never done business with adults. But dealer associations have been formed to try to stop dishonest sellers, so that collectors won't blame all dealers for problems created by a few.

Don't forget that dealers want to make a profit on what they sell. They hope to use the money for their own collections, or want to earn their living from cards. You're bound to meet a few "hard-sell" types (in this hobby, as in other walks of life) who want you to buy a lot, and buy it now!

And don't let dreams of getting rich push you into buying every new card set. "They're sure to go up in value," some dealers may say—about *all* the cards that they sell. Well, unless you want to be a dealer, too, why worry about that?

Here's another argument you'll hear: "Don't you want a *complete* collection?" Dealers might ask this if you're going to pass up buying an update set or another extra edition. But the idea of getting all the versions of sets issued by Topps or any other major manufacturer in a year is silly. Each card set is different. No company numbers all their cards from 1 to 10,000. No price guide reads, "All 15 Topps sets from 1991 for $1,000." Each set is a separate unit, numbered and valued individually.

You may feel sales pressure, too, when buying older cards. Cards in near-mint condition bring the highest prices, but they cost the most, too. Don't be embarrassed to ask a dealer for less-expensive grades of the same cards.

"Mint cards climb in value faster. Don't you want the best?" the dealer may ask.

Don't apologize for collecting VG-Ex cards (very good-to-excellent condition). Instead of hating the worn corner or small crease on a card, be proud you have something that has passed through so many hands. Consider your well-worn cards to be cardboard miracles that have survived lots of adventures.

Don't limit your hobby shopping to card shops and collector shows, either. Toy and department stores sell

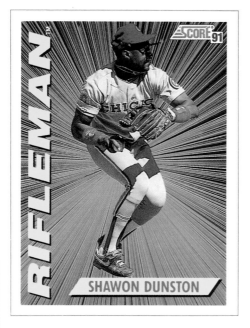

In the 1990s, companies began creating specialty cards for each year's edition. "Subsets," such as these from the 1991 Score set, seldom gain as much value as regular player cards, but their creativeness helps fill out 900-card sets.

lots of packs and sets, offering some bargain prices. Card dealers may raise prices immediately if price guides do, but stores tend to keep costs stable.

If you're hunting for bargains, the secret isn't merely knowing where to shop—it's knowing *when* to shop. Have you ever noticed how decorations, wrapping paper, and other holiday supplies go on sale after Christmas? The same timing is impor-tant when you are buying baseball cards.

The average dealer has only a limited amount of space on a hobby show table or in a shop to display merchandise. Dealers like to clear out a current year's cards at reduced prices after the baseball season ends. Many people lose interest in baseball after the World Series, reducing the demand for cards. Besides, the dealer will be receiving next year's cards in

EDDIE MURRAY 1B

KAL DANIELS

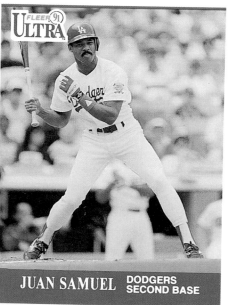

JUAN SAMUEL DODGERS SECOND BASE

Leaf (a relative of Donruss) was joined by the debut of Topps Stadium Club and Fleer Ultra in 1991. These are known as "high-end" or "premium" sets, due to their limited printings, added quality, and extra cost.

late December or early January. New cards will be more popular sellers. That means price reductions for old, individual packs.

Look at toy and chain stores for card bargains, too. Merchants who don't rely on cards for most of their income will sell discounted cards. Packs may be discounted by at least half, allowing the store owner a tiny profit. Sometimes, these massively discounted items are advertised and sold as "loss leaders": Even though the merchant won't make any profit on the "special" you buy, that sale item is intended to pull you into the store to buy higher-priced items.

Here's the best bargain of all: Each winter, as the holiday gift-giving season nears, card companies provide factory-sorted complete sets to large discount chains. In 1990, Score baseball sets were listed in price guides at forty to forty-five dollars. Meanwhile,

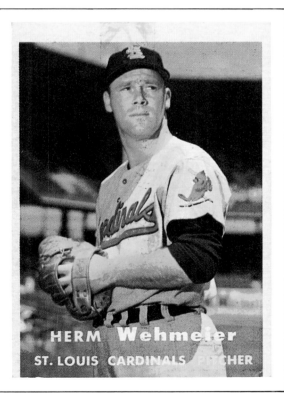

This 1957 Topps card receives a "poor to fair" grade, causing it to be virtually worthless. While the card has no major creases, none of the corners is still sharp. The photo isn't centered, causing poor card borders. Worst of all, the card is marred by gum stains and a bit of ancient cellophane tape.

chain stores were selling the same sets for approximately twenty dollars. How can that happen? Well, department stores can buy thousands of sets directly from the card-makers, obtaining the products at prices lower than dealers who buy smaller quantities.

Making the Grade

Before you buy your first card, or try to guess the value of your own growing collection, know how to grade cards. Card grades aren't like school grades. Instead, grading is the way hobbyists determine the condition of their cards.

School grades often mean the same thing from class to class. An "A" in English means you're at the top of the class. A "C" in math means that you're ranked in the middle, with lots of other people. But no one seems to agree on what card grades mean.

For most dealers and hobbyists, these guidelines meet most card-grading expectations:

Mint: The finest condition of card imaginable. All four corners are pointed and undamaged. The card is not faded, scuffed, scratched, or wrinkled. No printing flaws are seen. The photo is bright and well focused. The card is square, and all four borders are even. No gum or wax stains are found on the card.

Near-Mint: One tiny imperfection is seen on the card, only after close examination. These small problems could include one slightly bent corner or one uneven border.

Excellent: Maybe the photo on the card is off-center, or its once-glossy look is lost from constant handling. Corners will have minor wear. Still, cards in excellent condition won't have any creases or stains.

Very Good: Three or all four corners may be worn and round. The card may be slightly faded, with some small creases.

Good: Corners may show major wear. More bends and creases can be seen, yet any aging of the card has happened accidentally over time.

Fair: The card still looks rectangular but shows considerable damage, such as thumbtack holes, tape marks, writing, or tears. Deep creases may cause the cardboard to begin to separate.

Poor: The card has major damage. Sometimes, the card has been scribbled upon. Before update sets were created, kids used to write in new team names when a player was traded. Unpopular players would be defaced with mustaches or other cartoon-like features. Some practical collectors would punch large holes in cards and place them in three-ring binders. Sad but true.

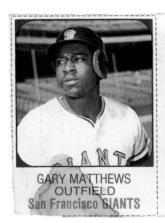

GARY MATTHEWS	FRED PATEK	MIKE LUM
OUTFIELD	INFIELD	INFIELD
San Francisco GIANTS	Kansas City ROYALS	Atlanta BRAVES

Box bottoms of Hostess snack cakes featured cards from 1975–1979. Many of the cards were damaged, either from rough handling at stores, from food grease seeping through boxes, or from collectors trimming out cards unevenly, damaging the borders.

In many cases, dealers will rank a card between two categories, calling it something like "VG-Ex" (very good to excellent). Sometimes the card's condition truly may rest between two levels. But sometimes these mid-ranges may be assigned to give a card a slightly better chance of gaining a higher price. Trying to judge the difference between a "poor" card and a "fair" one is like trying to decide how much salt is needed on French fries. Everyone has different tastes.

The most popular in-between category is "excellent-mint." Most price guides consider an Ex-Mt card to be worth about seventy-five percent of the near-mint price.

Note that price guides differ on grading expectations for various years of cards. Sets before 1980 will be listed starting at near-mint. After 1980, mint values are listed first. This is because the number of cards printed increased at that time. More cards were in circulation, so more could survive in mint condition.

Card conditions are debated constantly. If you try to sell a card to a dealer, it's likely that the dealer will put your card under a magnifying glass to find the smallest defect. The dealer may claim your card is in poor condition, even if it looks good to you. Why? Cards with lower grades are worth less.

On the other hand, you may meet dealers who make up grading terms like "gem mint." Look at those cards carefully. This could be an excuse to demand double the price-guide value by pretending the card has a special quality.

Read the above definitions carefully. Note that there are no exact guidelines observed by anyone in the hobby. That's why you need to examine individual cards carefully before buying.

Most of all, handle your cards with care. One little slip can add the smallest bend or scratch. That minor damage can drop your card a grade, which can lower its value immediately.

Keeping Cards Safe

Cards weren't meant to last forever. Their future health and value depend on you.

In the past, kids didn't think anything of storing their cards bundled in rubber bands. However, over the years, those rubber bands discolored the cards and sliced small grooves into the cardboard borders they held. This problem is known as "notching" by hobbyists.

Maybe an adult you know kept cards in a shoe box. As those cards bounced around loose, photos creased and corners bent.

To prevent unexpected card damage, be sure to save a portion of your hobby budget for storage supplies. One nine-pocket plastic sheet may sell for as little as a dime. That's a small price to pay to protect cards you've worked so hard to get.

A large three-ring notebook will be the perfect album for displaying your cards. When placing the cards in plastic sheets, slide each card slowly into the pocket. If corners get mashed in the process, you'll reduce the value of your cards.

If you're not working on a complete set, or if you acquire a really expensive card, think about a special holder. Various hard plastic frames and cases are available to protect just one card. These holders are clear, letting you view both sides of the card.

Each year, new products appear to help preserve and display cards. You'll find frames, cubes, and other devices just right for protecting and showing off your collection.

Because your cards are made of thin cardboard, they'll need protection from the elements. Be careful about keeping cards in basements, attics, or garages. Extreme hot, cold, or wet surroundings will damage them. Likewise, constant exposure to the sun or bright lights will fade your cards.

Remember that cards can be mangled even before you get them home.

Fleer issued numerous boxed sets in 1988, with each forty-four-card issue being distributed mainly through one retail chain. "League Leaders" was sold only through Walgreen drug stores.

Look into buying a plastic case or card box, something to keep cards flat and safe during trips.

Handle your cards carefully, but don't be afraid of them. Your sets won't explode! Even more important than future financial value is the enjoyment of your treasures today.

Hobby Homework

Finding newer cards at lower prices may be easy. Everyone, from hobby dealers to toy stores to grocers, sells packs and sets.

However, can you afford older cards? It's easy to guess that the sup-

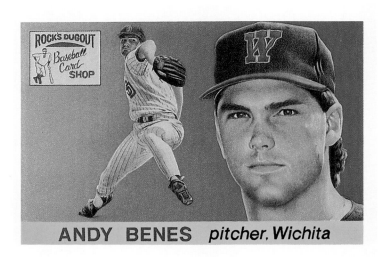

ANDY BENES *pitcher, Wichita*

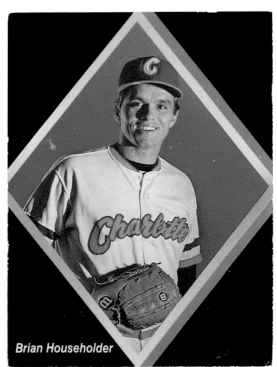

Brian Householder

During the 1980s, minor league players were featured in a variety of sets. Cards were sold only in team sets, stopping individual cards from gaining value.

plies of cards from twenty, thirty, or forty years ago have dried up. Hard-to-acquire vintage cards are often kept for a lifetime. To know exactly how valuable older cards might be, it's important to read a variety of price guides.

The most widely used, best-known price guide available is *Beckett Baseball Monthly.* This monthly magazine prices cards from 1948 to the present. Two value columns, a "low" and a "high," are presented for key cards from each set. If the "Beckett" lists a 1960 Carl Yastrzemski "rookie" card at $200 to $350, that means the price range varies in different parts of the country. Of course, sellers around Boston (or anywhere that dedicated Red Sox collectors are found) will get even more money for the card.

Does that mean a "Yaz" card would cost that much from a dealer? Not necessarily. Most price guides report surveys of the selling prices of certain cards. During the winter months, when no baseball is played, card values dip. Also, price guides overlook values for cards in less-than-perfect condition. A Yastrzemski card graded "excellent," with only one minor flaw, could sell for as little as half the amount listed. Any card with imperfections has a lower price tag.

Understand that the supply of older cards is reduced each year. No one is printing 1984 Donruss cards anymore. Cards from the 1950s and 1960s will be even harder to find. All these cards were made in much smaller quantities.

You can be sure that cards from the 1950s, 1960s, and 1970s will slowly and steadily grow in price. But cards from the 1980s and after may not. Because dealers have kept huge quantities of some sets, it's possible for a set to drop in value years after it's issued, when the stockpiles are released.

Furthermore, because more cards exist from the 1980s and 1990s, those card prices will remain lower longer. That's good news for buyers short of cash, but bad for sellers wanting to get rich quickly.

Some dealers may have "clearance" or "closeout" sales on certain products. Sale items will sell at incredibly cheap prices, with further discounts when you buy ten, fifty, or a hundred of the same item. Why? The dealer bought too many of those cards. He wants to get rid of them at any price (maybe even losing money) just to raise funds to buy new cards.

You won't see older cards from the 1960s and earlier dumped at unpredictable prices. Few dealers have the money and time needed to find and stockpile hoards of high-priced, hard-to-find oldies.

Now that you know how prized older cards are, here are a few tips on making vintage additions to your collection:

1. *Decide if you want quantity or quality.* You can buy a very-good-to-excellent condition set for half the price of a near-mint one. When it comes to individual cards from a twenty-year-old set, you can grab a hundred cards of unknown players for less than the cost of one star.

If complete sets from certain years seem unaffordable, consider starting a "type" collection. You could acquire just one card from each year, and have representatives from all the 1950s and 1960s sets. It would be like owning a small museum.

2. *Take star cards seriously.* Hank Aaron will always be considered one of the greatest sluggers in history, and Nolan Ryan will remain a great pitcher. Their permanent accomplish-

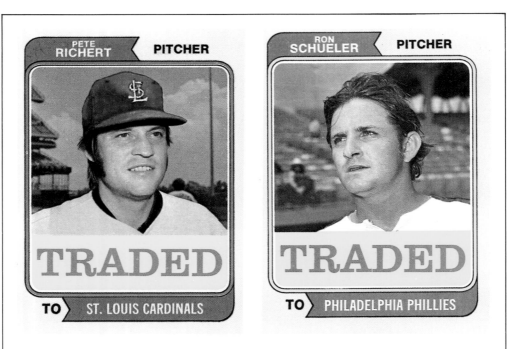

Before "traded" sets became a yearly tradition, Topps tried to issue a forty-three-card set in 1974. But instead of obtaining new photos, the company either painted new caps on old photos or depicted traded players without any team identification.

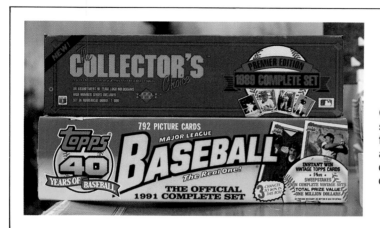

Card companies issue cards in complete factory-collated sets, allowing collectors to obtain everything in one purchase.

ments assure them lasting fame. That means retired superstars and Hall of Famers won't lose popularity, and neither will their cards. Even Pete Rose's trouble with the law, which got him banned from baseball, had only a temporary effect on his card values.

3. *Be willing to swap your newer cards for older cards.* And don't wait forever to buy the older cards you want, or they will pass you by. Maybe the prices of cards from the 1950s and 1960s increase only ten to twenty percent each year. However, how many of those old cards will you be able to find a year from now, at any price?

Vintage cards aren't for everyone, but learning about them will make you a wise and ready hobbyist. After some study, look at your own tastes and finances to decide what eras you want represented in your collection.

Setting Up Sets

Many collectors won't settle for just a few cards from a company in any chosen year. To them, the ultimate challenge is completing an entire set.

When collecting new card sets, you have a few choices. Here are some of your options:

1. *Buy factory-collated sets.* Since the 1980s, card companies have been willing to sell complete sets. This means that a company will sort all the cards for you, providing a complete set sealed in a special box.

Originally, collectors had to pay extra for this type of set. After all, someone else was doing the work of

Puzzle pieces are found in each foil pack of Donruss cards. The 1992 puzzle honored new Hall of Famer Rod Carew.

counting and sorting hundreds of cards for you. Now, all five major companies offer these sets to giant retail chains. Because these retailers purchase thousands of sets at once from the card-makers, customers can often buy factory-collated sets at prices much lower than any small hobby dealer could afford to charge.

The drawback here is that card manufacturers wait for months before offering factory-collated sets. If you collect new cards in the smaller foil packs, you'll have the editions nearly a half-year before the official complete sets are distributed.

2. *Hire some help.* Hobby dealers have found a way to compete with large department stores. Card-shop owners will assemble sets by hand, opening hundreds of foil packs and sorting the cards for you. If you want to be one of the first collectors to own a complete set of new cards, this is the route to take.

Buying a sorted-by-hand set has a

couple of advantages. First, you won't be stuck with duplicate cards. You'll own one, and only one, of each card made by the company that year.

Second, if you buy a set sorted by the neighborhood card seller, you can depend on follow-up service. If you buy a new factory-collated set from a chain store, you may be out of luck if it's missing a couple of cards, or if a few cards are miscut or damaged (it happens). At best, the store manager may tell you to write the manufacturer to complain. Your area hobby dealer, however, has taken the time to check each card beforehand. If a sorting mistake has occurred, that dealer can provide missing cards or replace defective ones immediately.

Of course, card dealers will ask more money for sets they assemble themselves. Because they spend hours opening packs and sorting the cards for you, they include their labor costs in the set price they charge.

3. *Pack it!* Although this method may be the least dependable, collectors can have the most fun and feel a real sense of accomplishment by building sets personally, one pack at a time.

Building sets by buying individual packs of cards takes luck, patience, and sometimes a few extra dollars. How many dollars? Get out your calculator for this question. Let's say that the imaginary Sweatsocks Gum Company produces a 900-card set. Each sixty-cent foil Sweatsocks package contains a fifteen-card assortment. Therefore, sixty packages could produce a complete set. The cost of collecting one set through packs would be thirty-six dollars, right?

Wrong! Companies don't promise that individual packs will produce a complete set. Cards are distributed randomly in packs, so you might have to buy a hundred packs—or even more—to get the complete Sweatsocks set. The odds aren't in favor of the collector in this case. Be prepared for lots of doubles, known in hobby language as duplicates or "dupes." Occasionally, you might get two of the same card in one package.

Why do collectors bother with packs, then? Most say it's because of the unexpected thrills that opening one package can bring. A dollar investment can yield a few hot cards worth five times that amount. Even if you get stuck with a hundred dupes while trying to complete your Sweatsocks set, those cards could be valuable trading or selling material. When you're willing to part with your extras, the per-pack cost of constructing a set will shrink. Your friends may be willing traders if they're working to complete the same set through packs.

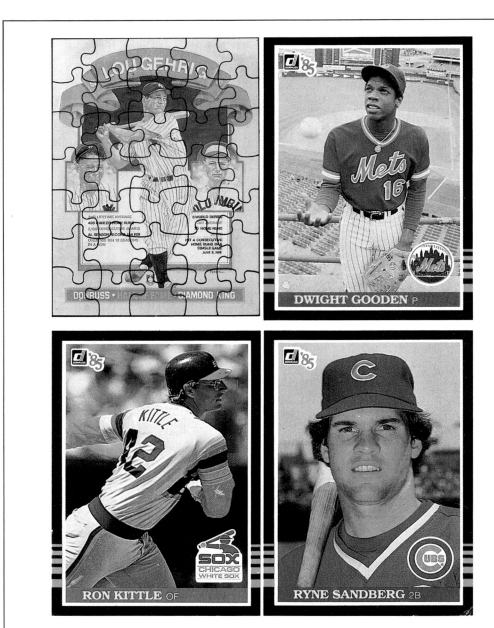

In the 1980s, companies experimented with placing panels of cards on the sides or bottoms of wax pack boxes.

Constructing your own set is a costly and time-consuming way to go, kind of like the difference between buying a house and building your own. Yet it remains a favorite in the hobby. A study of hobby habits by Action Packed Football Cards found that collecting through packs is an overwhelming choice among collectors. Of those studied, eighty-one percent said they buy packs for themselves, while only twenty-two percent buy complete sets.

Take a survey of your collecting friends. Chances are, do-it-yourself pack collecting will win out every time.

COLLECTOR SPECIALTIES

While many collectors focus on building sets, some look for specialties, such as rookie cards, star cards, and error cards. Even if you don't try to build a collection around them, these specialties can add excitement to the hobby.

Rookies

Ask twelve different collectors what a rookie card is, and you may get a dozen different answers.

The idea began in the 1970s, when Hank Aaron was surpassing Babe Ruth's all-time record of 714 home runs. Some hobbyists asked when Aaron appeared in a baseball card set for the first time—when he was a baseball card "rookie." That card was number 128 in the 1954 Topps set. It had not been extremely popular be-

The Yankees' 1991 first-round draft choice Brien Taylor (left) admires his card with Ken Goldin, executive vice president of Score Board, Inc. Classic Games signed the young pitcher and other draft picks to exclusive contracts, giving the company the right to issue the first-ever cards of the rookies.

fore Aaron's record-breaking 1974 season. Yet by 1981, Aaron's rookie card was listed in price guides at $125, considered a high price. A decade later, the card was valued at $1,200.

Before getting into the debate over what a rookie card is, remember what a rookie card *is not.* A rookie card is not necessarily rare. The Aaron rookie was actually among the easier-to-find cards back in 1954. Other cards, such as those numbered 51

through 75, seemed to be harder to get, possibly because Topps didn't distribute those particular cards to stores very well.

The reason a once-plentiful card can now be sold for $1,200 or more is that collectors like the idea of getting the player's first-ever card. The Aaron card and all other rookie cards are more popular than rare. Companies do not purposely print fewer cards of rookie players. These cards are randomly assigned to print sheets like

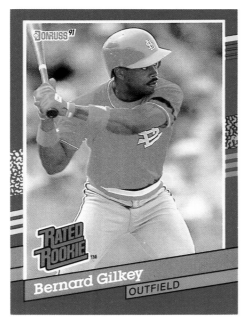

Beware! Just because a card might have a "rookie" label, don't assume that the player has never appeared in a card set before. Check price-guide magazines to discover a player's true first-ever card.

the others in the set. If rookie cards seem scarce, it is probably because they are in such high demand by collectors.

Collecting rookie cards of current players is easy. The difficult part is learning which cards should be considered "rookies."

In years when only Topps issued one baseball set, choosing was simple. Was the player making his first appearance on a baseball card?

That question is confusing. Five different companies—Topps, Fleer, Donruss, Score, and Upper Deck—produce numerous types of baseball sets throughout the year. Some new players may not appear in a company's larger set, but may be included in an updated edition issued after the end of the season. Could these cards be considered rookie cards?

Originally, all hobby authorities said no. Update, or "traded," sets were looked upon as separate sets. Besides, these season-ending sets were designed to be sold only through hobby dealers. If the cards weren't available to everyone at the same price through public sources (such as toy and department stores), then dealers would have the opportunity to control the supply and the price.

Things changed when Topps began offering "traded" cards on a test basis in wax packs. Because one fifty-cent pack offered just seven cards, few retailers could sell these. As a result, "traded" packs weren't available everywhere. Yet the guideline of being distributed through "dealers only" was no longer a way to test a rookie card's eligibility.

Upper Deck added another question to the rookie-card confusion. When the company began in 1989, it issued a 700-card set. Card numbers 701 through 800 were issued months later. These "high numbers" were available in two ways: as a complete subset from the factory or by being included in random foil packs.

Beckett Baseball Monthly noted the changing distribution patterns of cards. As a result, *Beckett* considers rookie cards from 1989 to the present to be the first card of a player issued in *any* set from a major manufacturer. Therefore, you'll see "RC" designations for cards from once-neglected secondary sets such as Fleer Update, The Rookies (by Donruss), or the Bowman set (by Topps). Confused? Many collectors share your frustration and have given up trying to master the rookie-card muddle.

Don't bet that you'll get rich gambling on rookie cards. Here's why they are so undependable. Suppose Hal Hotshot, an imaginary new player, is making his rookie-card appearance this year. If Hotshot makes the Yankees' starting lineup and hits .300 for the first half of the season, people may pay two dollars each for his cards, hoping he'll be a superstar.

What if he gets benched, is traded to a last-place team, or is sent to the minors? His card prices will drop instantly. On a week-to-week basis, a rookie's performance will be reflected in his current card values.

Ask some older collectors who J. R. Richard, Ron Kittle, or Joe Charboneau are. These three players were young hotshots who had short, disappointing careers. Collectors who had invested in hundreds of their rookie cards lost faith and money.

Of course, many adult collectors make an intense study of players who do well in college and the minor leagues, trying to get clues about which ones will be major-league stars. Even with this additional information, available in *USA Today* or *Baseball*

America, investing in rookies is like investing in the stock market. Both involve chance and possible losses.

From a historical point of view, rookie cards make sense. They are like seeing someone's baby pictures. From a financial standpoint, however, rookie cards remain risky business.

Seeking Stars

While rookie cards hold bigger financial rewards for investors, they bring bigger risks. Collectors wanting a sure thing look to star cards.

Unlike rookie cards, star cards have no strict definitions. In fact, any card of a famous player like David Justice or Roger Clemens will fit into the "star" card category. Visit a hobby shop or a card show, and you'll see that some dealers may sell only individual cards of well-known players.

Well-established performers are popular choices among star-card collectors. After seeing sluggers like Kirby Puckett, Barry Bonds, Jose Canseco, and Tony Gwynn succeed year after year, it's safe to say that their fame will be lasting. Each year, their cards may start selling at ten to twenty-five cents each, a step above cards of average players. (Cards of little-known athletes are called "commons" in the hobby.)

Each year, star cards may increase in value. But the amount may be only a dime or less, slightly more if your star participates in the All-Star game or helps his team reach the World Series. Occasionally, star cards may take temporary price dives. When players like Dwight Gooden and Wade Boggs faced drug abuse and other personal problems, the negative attention lowered their card values. However, when Gooden, Boggs, and some other sometimes-controversial players continued to excel on the field, their card values rebounded.

Star-card collectors face another problem when famed players are stuck on losing teams. The star may be blamed for his team's record, lessening his own appeal. Maybe the star plays for a small-city team, like the Montreal Expos or Houston Astros, where media coverage isn't as extensive. Without national media coverage, the star's cards may start to slip in price guides.

Think about it. The Dodgers, Angels, Mets, and Yankees seem to get more time on television, because they play in America's largest cities. The Cubs and the Braves are seen weekly across the country, thanks to faithful attention by cable TV. Players seen on the airwaves by millions each week will become popular baseball card subjects. Even so, smart card investors will judge star cards by the player's talent, not just by the popularity of his team.

Don't confuse star cards with those of hometown heroes. In Chicago, cards of Cubs or White Sox players may bring prices exceeding twice the price-guide listings. Why? Regional interest will lift card prices. Outfielder Andy Van Slyke's newest cards may bring fifteen to twenty-five cents each in Pennsylvania, because of his connection with the Pirates. However, California collectors following area teams like the Dodgers, Angels, Athletics, and Giants may find Van Slyke cards selling for less than a nickel.

You'll find dealers who ask the fairest prices for star players by looking at card shows and hobby publications. Out-of-state dealers may get cards of your local heroes at lower prices, and possibly pass that saving on to you.

Buying star cards will be easiest if you try to ignore trendy players. After

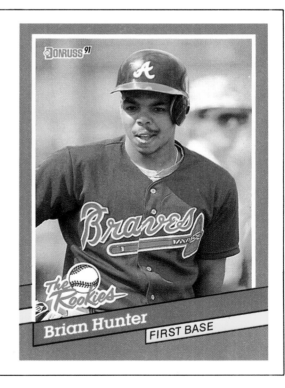

Since 1986, Donruss has issued a season-ending set saluting young players. Despite the title of the boxed set, the 56 cards aren't necessarily the first cards ever issued of those players.

a World Series, players who perform well will get temporary star status. Don't buy cards during post-season play, or after Most Valuable Player, Cy Young, and Rookie of the Year awards are presented. Buy cards of such "new" stars the next season. It's likely that these award-winning players won't be as successful the following year. If they decline even slightly on the field, their cards will be cheaper.

Some stars won't shine forever, because new players come along and beat the records of former greats. Yet some players rekindle their fame after retiring. For instance, Baltimore's Brooks Robinson wasn't the greatest-hitting third baseman in history. But he went on to become a recognized team announcer and popular hobby-show guest. This attention helped revive his card values. Other star players have become famous as coaches, or even actors or comedians.

The biggest boost for Robinson's cards came when he was elected to the National Baseball Hall of Fame in Cooperstown, New York. All his cards received instant price hikes of ten to fifty percent. Some collectors try to guess who will be elected to the Hall of Fame each year, buying before the good news increases values.

Remember that star cards are like rookie cards in that neither suffer from instant shortages. Collectors and dealers have given these cards a status and value based mostly on their popularity. If another player or another card becomes more popular, everything changes.

The Terror of Errors

Everyone makes mistakes, even baseball card companies. But when companies such as Fleer or Donruss make boo-boos, collectors who catch the blunders can make money.

Error cards are a popular but misunderstood part of the hobby. These cardboard oddities can be worth little or lots. The key is whether the company in error corrects the goof-up. When a corrected card is issued, collectors love trying to get both varieties of the card.

The most famous example of an error and how a company tried to fix it came in 1989. Fleer featured Baltimore's Billy Ripken on card number 616. Unknown to the company, the photo contained an easily seen obscene phrase written on the knob of Ripken's bat.

Fleer had already printed thousands of the naughty Ripken cards before discovering the glitch and racing to eliminate the cuss words. The company produced many variations of the card, trying to hide the vulgarity.

Upper Deck produced 2,500 cards honoring Ted Williams, including the limited editions in assorted 1992 foil packs. The Hall of Famer autographed and numbered each of the cards.

To this day, no Fleer officials have been willing to discuss how the offensive words were overlooked by the photographer and other company workers.

Because card companies won't tell just how many cards are printed each year, no one knows how many Ripken "errors" got into collector hands. Initially, dealers paid up to a hundred dollars apiece for the error card.

But three years later, collectors discovered that far fewer corrected versions (known as "variations" in hobby language) of the card were available. This means that Fleer must have caught the error near the end of their printing. In 1991 the Ripken card with the obscenity listed at five to ten dollars. The later card, which shows the questionable bat nob partially hidden by white paint, sold at twenty to thirty dollars.

The moral of this story: Error cards often lose value. Errors are often trendy, popular for only short periods of time. After their first public exposure, when everyone wants one of the cards, new sets with new mistakes will make hobby headlines.

The Ripken card mix-up also proved another point about errors. Sometimes, if a card company is late in fixing a mistake, few corrected cards will be printed. As a result, errors will be easier to get and less valuable; corrections will be fewer and more expensive.

Variations often occur when the printing of a set is flawed. In 1969 many of the names on the fronts of Topps cards appeared either in yellow or white. The white "variations" (thought to be cards that skipped the yellow printing process) are much harder to find, worth more than ten times the price of the same card with yellow lettering.

Many collectors don't bother looking for the tiny mistakes sometimes counted as errors. When price guides brag that some cards are worth more because their statistics were added wrong or a name was misspelled, some hobbyists get bored with the whole concept of error collecting. They feel that the error (and its corrected card counterpart) must feature either a major player or a major goof. The 1989 Upper Deck set met both needs with card number 357 of Dale Murphy. The first photo was flopped, or reversed, so that the writing on the uniform was backward. The correct version is worth fifty cents. The mistake is worth sixty to ninety dollars, partly because of Murphy's future as a potential Hall of Famer.

The most famous reversed photo may be from the 1957 Topps set: Home-run king Hank Aaron's card photo was printed backward! The result? He was incorrectly shown hitting left-handed, a goof that was never corrected.

Even unknown players can be the subjects of popular error and correction combinations. Fleer, in its 1988 set, botched card number 462 of Jerry Browne. Somehow, Fleer substituted a photo of white Texas teammate Bob Brower on the card of Browne, an African American infielder.

Normally, uncorrected errors don't increase in value. Topps never bothered to correct its 1969 card of California's Aurelio Rodriguez. The company photographer mistook the batboy for the infielder, putting the teenager on the player's card.

However, some classic tricksters have gained fame for their odd baseball cards. In 1959, Milwaukee Braves pitcher Lou Burdette pretended to be a left-hander for the camera. The fooled photographer didn't notice Burdette had a glove on the wrong hand.

These cards are great conversation pieces, fun things to tell other collectors about. That doesn't make them rarer than any other cards, so don't overpay for them. Normally, error cards are ignored by the majority of the collecting population. New error cards will slip in value when next year's mistakes appear. Don't get swept up in the excitement, buying errors just to compete with other hobbyists.

Just because a price guide lists an error card at five dollars, don't think you'll get ten dollars for it next year. Remember the "supply and demand" theory about cards? Even if your error card is in short supply, the demand has to be high for the card to resell.

SPECIAL SOURCES

Buying cards through hobby shops and retail stores isn't the only way to build your collection. If you're like most collectors, you'll want to seek out cards in other ways—by visiting hobby shows, trading, buying through the mail, and looking in unusual places.

Surviving Hobby Shows

Collectors young and old feel excitement when attending a hobby card show, one of those weekend events held in church basements, hotel ballrooms, shopping malls, or other public places. Anywhere from a half-dozen local dealers to several hundred merchants from many states gather to sell their collectibles. The annual National Sports Collectors Convention draws tens of thousands of collectors, who come to view some eight hundred tables piled high with old and new cards.

Don't be overwhelmed by the size and scope of card shows. With some patience and planning, you'll be able to bring home some bargain-priced cardboard treasures.

First, find the hobby events nearest to you. Read the sports section of your local newspaper, and ask workers at nearby hobby shops about upcoming shows. And remember to read the show listings in hobby magazines.

When you can arrange a visit to a hobby show, allow yourself a couple of hours to shop and study. No one would rush through Disneyland without having time to take some rides. Hobby shows have almost as many attractions, so try not to hurry through a showroom.

Notice how the first two tables near the entrance of a hobby show seem to do the most business. Many collectors panic, thinking that no cards will be left by the time they view everything. So they buy the first things they see.

Wrong! Perhaps, at the far end of the room, some dealers are willing to sell their cards for less. Fewer customers seem to be walking past their tables, so they want to create more business.

Most of all, if you're shopping for certain cards from your favorite sets and don't see them on display, don't be shy about asking dealers if they sell those items. A dealer may have only eight feet of space to display thousands of cards. You're likely to find only the smallest or most expensive cards on display, to allow the dealer more chance for profit. However, if you ask, it's possible that the dealer may have boxes of commons or cheaper-priced sets stacked out of sight under or behind the table.

When it's time to make your purchase, realize that dealers may be willing to accept slightly lower prices.

True! Veteran collectors enjoy negotiating lower prices with all dealers. The fine art of dickering has several keys:

1. *Never negotiate in a crowd.* No dealer will offer you a discount with a crowd of customers at the table. Soon, other customers will be yelling "Me, too!" Everyone will want lower prices.

2. *Be reasonable.* Don't expect a dealer to sell you a five-dollar card for a dime. However, if you're buying twenty dollars worth of cards, many sellers will grant a ten percent discount. The more you buy, the better your chances will be for lower prices.

Also, accept small victories and defeats. If a dealer agrees to sell a dollar

When attending hobby shows, many companies give free samples to visiting collectors. Sheets like these are valuable collectibles, especially if marked with a mintage number (such as "1 of 20,000").

card for fifty cents, don't keep trying to get the price down to a nickel. The dealer might feel cheated and call the deal off.

If you strike out trying for a lower price, thank the dealer for listening. Then move on. You tried your best. Even superstars don't succeed every time.

3. *Look for mysteries.* Examine a dealer table. Is the dealer selling only one type of product? For example, if Harry Hobbydealer sells nothing but singles from 1993 sets, then his one 1981 Donruss set on the table seems out of place. Chances are he hasn't been able to sell the set, and he may dump it at nearly any price.

Find the oddball cards that don't seem to go along with the merchandise a dealer sells. Then move in for a hobby markdown.

4. *Time your deal.* Study the pace of a show. Is everyone buying and selling cards, or is there a deadly quiet? Plan on negotiating when business is slowest.

Each collector has a different strategy for dickering with dealers. Some dealers are anxious to make a few sales during the opening hour of a two-day show. If you're the first customer of the day willing to buy, ask for a lower price. The dealer may agree, knowing that you're making his table seem like a busy, interesting place to shop.

On the other hand, some dealers may not take a penny less for anything at a weekend show. They won't change until it's time to close on Sunday afternoon. Suddenly, you appear at the table moments before the show ends. The dealer, unwilling to pack up and carry extra boxes back home, agrees. Some profit is better than no profit.

Of course, some dealers compare themselves to a supermarket manager or restaurant owner, and believe that they should never reduce prices on any items for anyone. Don't argue with them. After all, they've worked many hours. Renting tables and buying showcases for their cards are but two of the expenses that dealers have, so they may be unwilling to give up any of their profits. Instead of de-

That's a baseball card? The 1991 Topps Stadium Club set included an unusual photo of then-Oakland pitcher Eric Show out of uniform. In the off season, Show is a professional guitarist.

bating, find another dealer who is more anxious for your business.

But don't get so caught up in shopping and bartering that you forget to enjoy the show. Here's your opportunity to view thousands of cards up close and in color. Politely ask questions, and any worthwhile dealer will gladly share hobby knowledge with you.

That's the best hobby bargain of all.

Trades

When it comes to cards, buying and selling aren't your only choices. Trading is also a possibility. While the art of swapping is tougher today than ever before, it's still possible for two people to make deals without any money.

Trades aren't risky, as long as you study card values first. You'll find dealers and even other collectors who'll test your knowledge. You'll meet people who'll try to get the better end of a deal. So the first rule to observe in face-to-face trades is simple: Keep a current price guide handy. No one should be expected to make one-sided trades without understanding what's happening.

The second rule may be a bit confusing at first, but it's true, anyway: Be willing to make a bad trade. Lose to win.

How's that?

Let's try an example. Suppose you have a card of Will Clark worth fifty cents. Will you make a mistake trading that for two rookie cards priced at fifteen cents each?

Not necessarily. True, you've sacrificed a card of an established star— but this star has also had some disappointing seasons. Meanwhile, those low-priced cards of your unknown rookie could skyrocket if he helps his team to a first-place finish. See how it works? A little loss now could mean a big win later.

This is only one instance where taking a lower return value in a trade now can help you in the future. Could trading a three-dollar card for a buck's worth of commons be a good idea? Maybe. If those commons help you complete a set, you'll be gaining more than three dollars for your efforts. Thinking about long-term benefits is the best way to get a worthwhile trade.

After you read magazines and books like this, you'll be prepared to be a wise trader. Don't be too wise, though.

You'll meet new collectors who are anxious to make *any* trades. They won't be concerned about card values, so you could have the chance to cheat them. You could exchange a pile of worthless, boring cards for boxes of big-ticket stars or rookies.

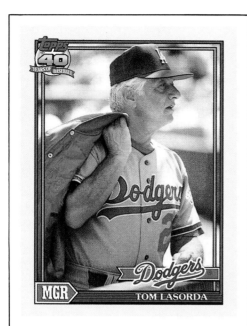

For years, Topps has been the only company willing to produce cards of team managers. Shown is a 1991 example.

Why should you be honest? Although making unfair trades may not seem like stealing, it's not that different. Some collectors may be so upset at being cheated, they'll drop out of the hobby. Others will be angry, and will try to take advantage of more newcomers. "What goes around, comes around" is an old saying that in this case means you might create cheaters who will try to trick you in the future.

If you talk to people who have been collecting cards for a few years, they'll tell you about the friends they've made during that time. Being kind to new hobbyists is a perfect way of making lasting friends. While cardboard may not last forever, a friendship can.

When you give other collectors a good deal in a trade, tell them they can make it up to you next time. Better yet, tell them to be nice to the next person when they trade again. When fairness becomes contagious, baseball card collecting can become the best hobby ever.

Collecting by Mail

Anyone, anywhere, can collect baseball cards. While it would be ideal to live next door to a card shop or around the corner from a weekly hobby show, your location doesn't have to be a problem.

Thanks to the postal service, collectors can buy, sell, or trade by mail. With a few stamps and a little bit of shopping, it's possible to save time and money.

Dealers selling by mail may offer some great deals. Why?

First, they don't have to worry about costs that shop owners face, such as store rent and employee wages. Second, mail-order dealers don't spend lots of money and hours traveling to

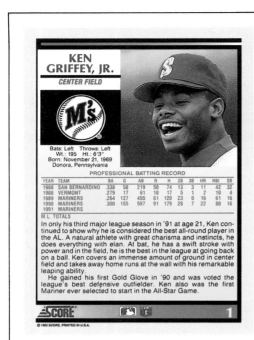

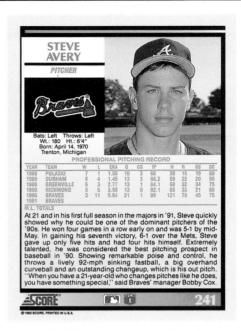

Look closely at the stats on these 1992 Score cards. The company produced these samples before the 1991 season was over, in order to preview the new card design. However, stats were unavailable for the unfinished season. These "prototypes" were distributed only to the media and hobby dealers.

hobby shows to set up and operate tables. If dealers spend less, they can charge customers less.

When you order cards from a magazine advertisement, you'll notice that a dealer charges extra money for "postage and handling." Even if you order only one card, you might be paying a dollar or more in extra charges.

Believe it or not, that's fair. Sure, postage may not account for all of the extra fees. However, smart dealers know that cards must be wrapped well, to avoid being damaged in the mail. Padded envelopes, plastic card holders, or thick cardboard boxes may be part of the "handling" cost. And dealers define "handling" as including the time needed to wrap and send your package. In other words, the extra cost is partially a labor charge.

Following are a few rules for customers to follow whenever collecting by mail.

1. *Never send cash by mail.* When you send cash, there's no receipt or proof of your payment. If you don't get the cards you ordered, there's no way of proving that you paid. Instead, have an adult write a personal check for you. Or ask at your bank or post office about obtaining a cashier's check or money order. These methods are safer if your letter gets lost or if you want a refund or exchange.

2. *Learn the rules.* If the cards you ordered aren't available, how will you get a refund? Some mail-order dealers like to give credit slips, meaning that you have to buy other merchandise instead of getting your money returned.

What if you don't like the cards you ordered, or they aren't what you expected? Maybe the cards aren't in mint condition as promised. How soon do you have to return the cards for a refund? Can you send the cards back, trading them for something else?

If you don't discover these answers in the ad, write to the dealer. Any dealer unwilling to answer your questions is unworthy of your business.

3. *Check out the seller.* Many hobby periodicals have customer service departments, which investigate complaints against advertisers. Dealers who keep a spotless record are awarded customer service awards. These are "seals of approval," indicating that you can order without worry.

Or try running your own test. Make a small purchase from a dealer. If your cards arrive as described, promptly and in good condition, then you can try purchasing more from the same person.

Most people who do business by mail are just like you—honest types who aren't able to reach lots of other collectors in person. Don't be worried about an advertiser just because the only return address is a post office box.

Many people once believed that only crooks rented post office boxes, in order to keep their real addresses and identities secret. Actually, the United States Postal Service requires anyone doing business at a P.O. box to list his or her permanent location on a rental form. Then, if you do have a consumer problem, the post office can help you locate the person running "Yards of Cards," or some other oddly named dealership that doesn't reveal the names of the people in charge.

4. *Keep a file of your purchases through the mail.* Save the original ad you answered, along with the receipt of your purchase.

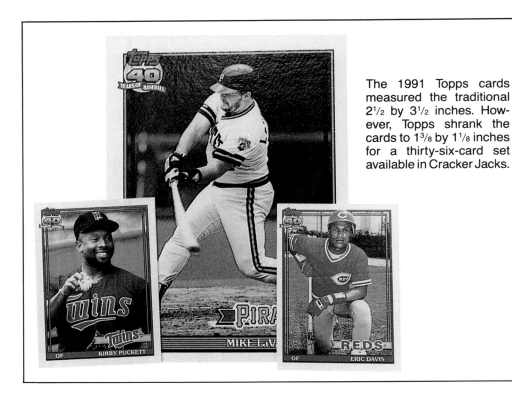

The 1991 Topps cards measured the traditional 2½ by 3½ inches. However, Topps shrank the cards to 1⅜ by 1⅛ inches for a thirty-six-card set available in Cracker Jacks.

Why? There is a possibility that dishonest people are doing business by mail, just as dishonest people can run stores. Before saying you've been cheated, contact the mail-order dealer once more. Sometimes, a dealer can make a simple mistake, or get behind in answering customers.

However, if a dealer really tries to cheat you, there is something you can do. Postal fraud is a federal crime. Contact your local postmaster and ask about filling out a complaint form.

Next, contact the publication that ran the ad you responded to. Write to the advertising manager of that magazine, sending photocopies of the correspondence you've had with the dealer.

Don't let these cautions discourage you. Most people will have no problems buying, selling, or trading by mail. These collectors avoid the hassles and expense of traveling to card shows and shops by letting the cards come to them.

Buried Treasures

Baseball cards can be found everywhere, sometimes at incredibly low prices. But finding *great* cards at low prices can be harder than digging for buried treasure. Don't depend on the usual hobby and retail markets for cards. Try imagining some out-of-the-way outlets for surprise collectibles.

Flea markets and antique shops may have older cards, but their prices may be even higher than price-guide estimates. Instead, whenever possible, search out garage sales, thrift shops, and other places where used items are sold.

Have you tried looking for cards in your own neighborhood? Maybe even within your own family? Ask friends, family, and neighbors to help you look for cards. Have your aunts, uncles, cousins, and grandparents search

their attics and basements. Spread the word. Many adults may not realize what you collect. Or they may believe you wouldn't be interested in anything but cards of current players, not wanting "old" ones for your collection.

Some adult collectors spend lots of money advertising their desire to get more cards. One of the best ways you can advertise is free. It's known as "word of mouth." Tell everyone about your collection. Give speeches in class about the hobby. Write reports about cards. The news of your pastime will spread quickly.

Cards won't come knocking on your door. You have to search for them. However, when you find them for free, or at low prices, they make your collection even more meaningful. You'll love the stories of your card-hunt adventures almost as much as the cards themselves.

HOBBY HURDLES

As you build your collection, you'll encounter new situations. You may have a chance to have one of your cards autographed. How will that affect its value? You may want to sell some of your cards to raise money for your hobby. How can you get the best price? You'll come across deals that seem too good to be true and cards that may be counterfeit. How can you avoid being "taken"?

Autographs

Even if you don't collect autographs, the idea of getting your cards signed by baseball celebrities is tempting. On the surface, autographs can seem like great investments. You might have to spend twenty dollars or more to get a Hall of Famer like Rollie Fingers or a current hero like Dwight

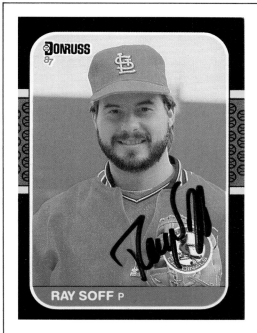

RAY SOFF P

KEN HOWELL P

Autographed cards may lessen in value, unless the cards are resold to autograph collectors. Hobby purists would claim that these cards are no longer mint because they've been damaged by handwriting.

Gooden to sign one of your cards at a hobby show.

So, if you have a Joe Superstar card worth five dollars, will spending another twenty dollars for an in-person autograph make a twenty-five dollar collectible? Not necessarily. No price-guide book exists for auto-graphed cards, meaning that the worth of your card will be hard to pin-point. In fact, some collectors would insist that your signed card has lost value.

Yes, it's true. Do you remember the definition of a mint-condition card? Well, isn't an autographed card marred by handwriting?

Here's the problem: Only auto-graph collectors will agree that your card has a greater value. And even autograph hobbyists will debate how much that new value is.

Just because a show promoter charges you twenty dollars for the right to obtain a single autograph from the visiting star, there's no guarantee that the autograph is worth that much. Therefore, don't spend a lot of money to gain autographed cards, especially if profit is your only aim. If you do want to get cards signed, here are a few tips to help preserve the value of the cards:

1. *Never have valuable cards autographed.* Choose easier-to-find cards with smaller values. Why? You won't be risking the future of your best rookie and star issues that way. Instead of breaking up sets, try to use your extras for autographs.

2. *Use a Sharpie.* When autograph collectors buy cards, they like to have cards signed in blue Sharpie. This is a permanent marking pen, which costs about a dollar anywhere that school supplies are sold. Sharpies make it easy for stars to write a bold, even signature on the slick surface of a card. Though the mark is permanent, be sure to allow a few minutes of drying time after the signing. Even a Sharpie autograph will smear if touched before it's dry.

3. *Know the trends of autographing.* No collectors, autograph hounds or otherwise, want cards personalized (like "To Stinky"). Also, cards signed in felt-tips, pencils, or faint, weird colors, aren't popular. Most of all, *never* have a card signed on its back. Collectors want the autograph and front picture together.

Card collectors outnumber other types of collectors, which means you decrease the number of buyers for your cards when autographs are included. Then again, will you ever want to sell your autographed cards? If getting a famous signature was a fun, exciting experience, you might not trade that memory for all the money in the world.

Selling

Cards cost money. Paying for cards and supplies is one of the biggest challenges that card collectors face.

Most young hobbyists depend on allowances, gifts on special occasions, or part-time jobs to raise funds for cards. However, with an active hobby market in your favor, it's possible to pay for some of your hobby by selling cards. All you need is a price guide and some enthusiasm.

Don't assume that your local card-shop dealer is the greatest customer for your extras. Even though your price guide says you have a five-dollar stash of cards in your hands, you may not get half that amount in cash from the shop owner.

Why not? To begin with, that shop owner only *sells* cards at the price-guide values. Most dealers pay no more than half "book" value for cards, in order to make a profit. After all,

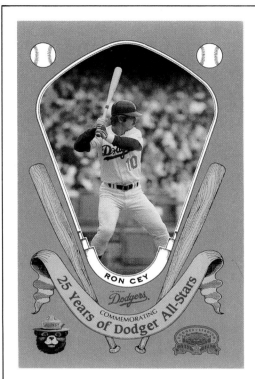
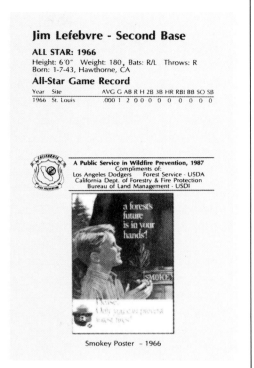

Jim Lefebvre - Second Base

ALL STAR: 1966

Height: 6'0" Weight: 180, Bats: R/L Throws: R
Born: 1-7-43, Hawthorne, CA

All-Star Game Record

Year	Site	AVG	G	AB	R	H	2B	3B	HR	RBI	BB	SO	SB
1966	St. Louis	.000	1	2	0	0	0	0	0	0	0	0	0

A Public Service in Wildfire Prevention, 1987
Compliments of:
Los Angeles Dodgers   Forest Service - USDA
California Dept. of Forestry & Fire Protection
Bureau of Land Management - USDI

Smokey Poster – 1966

Many team-issued cards, especially those given free to fans at the ballpark, have sponsors. In 1987, the U.S. Forest Service helped print a forty-card set for the Los Angeles Dodgers. Past and current Dodger All-Stars were shown, while a safety tip from Smokey Bear was on each card back.

dealers have store expenses, like rent, advertising, and electricity, as well as the overall need to earn a living.

Besides, that dealer may already have a pile of cards just like yours. You have to think about supply and demand now, just as dealers do.

You'll get top prices for your cards when demand is high and supplies are low. Suppose that you have some current cards of New York Mets and Yankees players. If you live on the East Coast, demand for these cards will be high because the teams are popular locally. When lots of people want and buy the same cards, the supply shrinks. When supply is low, people are willing to pay more money.

Now suppose that you have the

same Mets and Yankees cards, but you live in California. Fans there are much more interested in the Athletics, Dodgers, Angels, Giants, and Padres. Card shops probably have a lot of Mets cards just like yours, and can't sell them no matter how cheap the price.

Perhaps you dream of making easy money investing in cards. For only one dollar, you can take a low-priced hobby gamble.

Think about who will be the top teams and players in one year. Then, make your picks. Maybe you can buy five twenty-cent rookie cards, or ten semi-stars for a dime each. If you're a mind reader, try finding twenty commons at a nickel each.

As the season continues, monitor the price guides. Are your investments gaining value? When the prices start climbing, sell off some of your stock to regain your dollar investment. For instance, if your dime cards have reached the twenty-five-cent mark, sell off four of them. You've recouped your buck, and have six more cards to sell later, possibly at higher values.

Be ready for your scheme to backfire, too. Maybe that promising pitcher you invested in had a career-ending shoulder injury. Stranger things have happened.

Because risk is involved when investors try to sell, sensible collectors focus on selling doubles, or extra cards no longer needed. In any case, know that you won't make a fortune with every card you sell. After all, no batter belts a homer each trip to the plate.

Counterfeits and More

Valuable baseball cards have been counterfeited on many occasions, causing worries for collectors.

In 1991, Leaf-Donruss struck back against two men accused of illegally reproducing 1990 Leaf cards of Frank Thomas. At the time, the actual cards were bringing seventy-five dollars each. However, dealers were buying up bundles of the bogus Thomas cards at twenty-five dollars each. The men were stopped and charges of fraud were filed.

The Thomas forgeries were better than most counterfeits. In many instances, collectors who have any legitimate card from a set can detect the phony. If you can hold both cards in your hand, you might feel the difference. Card companies are very selective about choosing the right "stock," the proper type and thickness of cardboard to print on.

Your eyes may discover other clues to counterfeits. Look at both cards. The actual card should be more clear and colorful. Sometimes, a counterfeiter omits one color, or simply reprints a photo of the real thing.

Counterfeits, however, aren't the biggest problem that hobbyists face. A few dishonest people have found sneakier ways to trick collectors.

In 1990 some people were selling Upper Deck "error" cards on which the player's position was not printed on the card front. Such "error" cards could be created simply by rubbing an eraser briskly over the card front to remove the type.

Suppose that, at a card show, you see older cards from the tobacco era going for unbelievably low prices. Such cards may actually be from commemorative reprint sets. The cards can be "aged" by crumpling or other methods. The small print on the card back reading "reprint" is removed in a related sneaky fashion. Then the dishonest seller claims that the worn condition of the card is why the price is so affordable.

One of the oldest tricks in hobby history is the black-and-white "proof" card. The story goes that a company made early versions of popular cards in black and white. These alleged "prototypes" can be created on a photocopy machine. The actual cards are reproduced for pennies and then resold as priceless rarities.

If you think counterfeit cards might be hard to tell from the real thing, how about imaginary cards? These cards, sometimes described as "retro" cards, are issued years after an event took place.

In the 1980s some tricksters suddenly found high school cards depicting Yankee star Don Mattingly. These cards would sell for five to twenty-five dollars apiece, maybe more to an avid fan. The problem: This was a one-card "set" that never happened. Without the player's permission, someone crudely reproduced a photo of a young Mattingly printed in *Sports Illustrated*. Then the mystery cards started appearing at ridiculous prices.

Other popular stars have been the subjects of such schemes. Maybe a card shows Will Clark in his Olympic uniform, or Darryl Strawberry in the minors. Of course, these cards are crudely made, having no identifying printer's or sponsor's name on the back.

Here's another tip to help expose questionable cards: Ask what set the card is from. One-card "sets" normally don't exist. Can the dealer tell you the history of the set, or what happened to the other cards? Is the set listed in any guides?

Unlicensed cards are another kind of trickery. These may be attractive, colorful cards. However, they aren't part of a real set. Instead, they are produced for many years. These cards don't pay royalties to the players shown, nor to the teams whose symbols are seen.

Education can fight tricks like this. Don't bet that a dealer will offer you a one-of-a-kind card at a bargain price. Veteran collectors enjoy repeating the old saying, "If something sounds too good to be true, it probably *is* too good to be true."

Often, the greediest people are the easiest to cheat. Someone hoping to get a billion-dollar card for a few bucks will believe anything. These people need to shop by using their heads, not their wild imaginations.

Deceptions begin in one region of the country, but spread when traveling dealers unsuspectingly buy bunches of the questionable cards. Hobby publications are honest in reporting counterfeits and other faked cards. Keep reading, and you might be warned of potential problems.

Don't let the worry of buying phony cards scare you away from collecting. Collect for fun and not for profit. After all, who would take the time to counterfeit a widely available card that is worth only a few cents?

Slick Sales Pitches

Collectors may have to contend with trick pitches thrown by dealers and other merchants. At a hobby shop, card show, or chain store, you're likely to find misleading offers. Everyone wants to resell common-priced cards at a fat profit.

The biggest offender here is the pre-packaged "assortment." Supermarkets and other retail stores offer card packs hanging from shelf pegs. Flashy labels will make meaningless promises like "100 different pro baseball cards." The top card may be a semi-star worth up to a quarter. Buyers get fooled, thinking that lots of star cards are hiding underneath.

Think again. That assortment pack, despite its fancy wrapping, probably has cards worth less than a nickel each. The retail per-card price likely is two to three times the actual value of the mix of cards.

Maybe you'll bump into the promise of instant card riches near the exit of your favorite chain store, where, among those familiar gumball dispensers, another coin-eating machine waits.

Some machines promise only two cards for a quarter, but have valuable cards displayed in their windows. How about getting a rookie card of Ken Griffey Jr. for a quarter? Dream on! These machines don't make guarantees. If you get a pair of cards worth a dime, that's too bad. Don't think you'll get your quarter back, either.

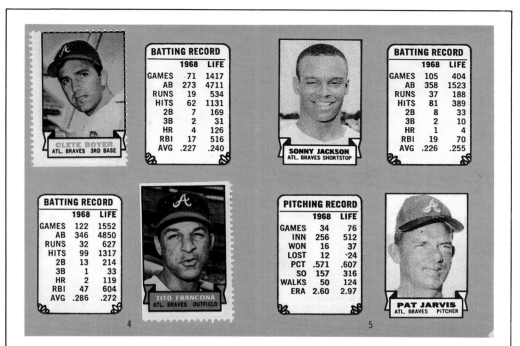

BATTING RECORD		
	1968	LIFE
GAMES	71	1417
AB	273	4711
RUNS	19	534
HITS	62	1131
2B	7	169
3B	2	31
HR	4	126
RBI	17	516
AVG	.227	.240

CLETE BOYER
ATL. BRAVES 3RD BASE

SONNY JACKSON
ATL. BRAVES SHORTSTOP

BATTING RECORD		
	1968	LIFE
GAMES	105	404
AB	358	1523
RUNS	37	188
HITS	81	389
2B	8	33
3B	2	10
HR	1	4
RBI	19	70
AVG	.226	.255

BATTING RECORD		
	1968	LIFE
GAMES	122	1552
AB	346	4850
RUNS	32	627
HITS	99	1317
2B	13	214
3B	1	33
HR	2	119
RBI	47	604
AVG	.286	.272

TITO FRANCONA
ATL. BRAVES OUTFIELD

4

PITCHING RECORD		
	1968	LIFE
GAMES	34	76
INN	256	512
WON	16	37
LOST	12	·24
PCT	.571	.607
SO	157	316
WALKS	50	124
ERA	2.60	2.97

PAT JARVIS
ATL. BRAVES PITCHER

5

Back in 1969, Topps printed 240 stamps of players, along with 24 team albums. Each stamp measured 1 by 1$^{7}/_{16}$ inches.

Trickier traps may wait at hobby shops or card shows. The worst of these come-ons has to be games of chance.

Pay anywhere from twenty-five cents to a dollar. Then you'll throw dice or twirl a spinner. "Everyone's a winner!" is the false promise that lures many collectors into losing. Maybe you'll win something, but will you win cards equal to the cost of playing the game?

To their credit, many large-show promoters forbid table-holders to offer games of chance. Yet these carnival-like temptations may appear in small shows, flea markets, and hobby shops.

You could face the same unhappy ending spending a dollar or more on a "grab bag." Some dealers stick unwanted, non-selling cards in bags. Don't listen to stories of how a guy just got a ten-dollar card. Putting blind trust into farfetched schemes isn't a great way to find a bargain.

A smaller hobby hurdle facing collectors is called the "brick." Dealers will offer a bunch of cards (the hobby term comes from the shape of the card pile), possibly with a label like "1987 Topps, 100 cards." Here's the sales pitch: The assortment is priced cheaply, maybe even at less than half of the price-guide value for that many cards.

Don't look at the valuable card appearing on the front of the bundle. Don't figure how much money you might save.

Instead, ask these questions of the seller:

1. *Are all the cards different?* When someone says "100 assorted," that could mean you're getting four each of twenty-five different cards.

2. *Are all the cards the same grade?* Just because a mint-condition card is seen on the top of the stack, don't assume that all the other cards are shipshape, too.

Assortments can be great ways to start sets at a lower cost. Some dealers don't want to take the time to put thousands of inexpensive cards in numerical order, knowing that their time and energy could be wasted on uninterested customers. Instead, making "bulk" sales allows dealers to lower their costs. The key is to understand what you're buying, so that you won't be disappointed.

One of the worst examples of how card assortments are misrepresented can be found on cable TV shopping programs or in non-hobby magazine advertisements. High-pressure commercials trick listeners into thinking they are getting complete sets. Instead, dealers have "cherry picked" sets, meaning that all the valuable star and rookie cards have been removed beforehand. Pay close attention, and you'll never find the words "complete set" used in deceptive sales.

There's no need to be suspicious of every hobby dealer you meet. Many adult dealers remember how they started collections when they were your age. They may feel that if you are happy buying cards from them when you're young, you'll want to remain a steady buyer when you're older.

Still, now that you "know the score" regarding possible hobby hurdles, you're a capable customer. Dealers should be happier dealing with someone who has studied beforehand.

Knowledge is power in the hobby. Ask other collectors to suggest dealers who are fair and helpful; then pass along the information to other newcomers. When collectors stick together, they can overcome any challenges.

NEWS AND VIEWS

Once you become an active collector, you'll want to stay active. Reading hobby-related magazines and books is the best way to keep informed of changes in the card market. You can also get information through the mail.

Hobby Publications

Newsstands and hobby shops carry many different magazines for card collectors. Here are some interesting choices.

Baseball Cards magazine (700 East State Street, Iola, WI 54990): A monthly, *Baseball Cards* contains humorous, fresh examinations of hobby issues. Past features have included a series that detailed card shops and other hobby landmarks in numerous American cities.

Beckett Baseball Monthly (4887 Alpha Road, Suite 200, Dallas, TX 75244): This magazine remains a tradition with all ages of collectors, thanks to its popular price guide. When collectors say they pay "Beckett," they mean they buy cards at the prices listed in this magazine.

Sports Collectors Digest (700 East State Street, Iola, WI 54990): *SCD* is published by Krause Publications, the same company responsible for *Baseball Cards*, *Baseball Card News* (published twice monthly), and other publications for card collectors. *SCD* is published weekly and reports on all types of sports memorabilia, providing immediate news of new products, card-value changes, and other happenings. Issues often contain more than 300 pages. At least seventy-five percent of the space is filled with advertisements, giving hobbyists a large catalog to shop through. *SCD* isn't the most helpful publication for a beginning collector, but adults who have collected for years wouldn't do without it.

Topps Magazine (254 36th Street, Brooklyn, NY 11232): This quarterly magazine is published by Topps, the same company that prints numerous card sets each year. That can be good or bad, depending on your view. In each issue, Topps inserts special cards and posters that make the price of the magazine a bargain. But because Topps owns the magazine, you won't read about other companies' sets.

Along with magazines, new books about the hobby appear each year. The most common type of book is the annual price guide. Think twice, however, about buying this kind of reference. The lists of past sets are helpful, especially when it comes to regionals or smaller sets ignored by many dealers. The prices, though, may be out of date by the time you turn the first page.

Here's an example: Price-guide books once considered Pete Rose cards hotter than hot. After he was suspended from baseball for life, prices plunged in one week. However, the books were inaccurate for months.

Sometimes the price changes will be small ups or downs. Still, to be accurate, it's important to get price-guide magazines for current news. Following are a few books that may be especially helpful for new collectors:

Baseball Cards: Questions and Answers, by Sports Collectors Digest

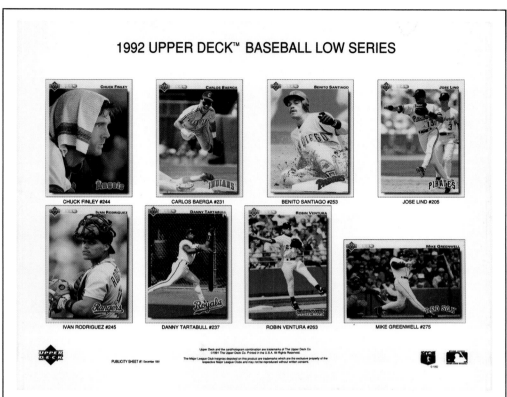

1992 UPPER DECK™ BASEBALL LOW SERIES

CHUCK FINLEY #244

CARLOS BAERGA #231

BENITO SANTIAGO #253

JOSE LIND #205

IVAN RODRIGUEZ #245

DANNY TARTABULL #237

ROBIN VENTURA #263

MIKE GREENWELL #275

PUBLICITY SHEET #1 December 1991

Upper Deck and the card/hologram combination are trademarks of The Upper Deck Co.
©1991 The Upper Deck Co. Printed in the U.S.A. All Rights Reserved.
The Major League Club insignias depicted on this product are trademarks which are the exclusive property of the
respective Major League Clubs and may not be reproduced without written consent.

Months before new sets are available, companies like Upper Deck distribute preview cards and photos. Because these are given only to hobby dealers and the media, these promotional items may be expensive or hard to find.

(Krause Publications): An assortment of questions submitted by all levels of collectors. Short, simple answers on lots of subjects give readers an encyclopedia of card knowledge.

Sports Americana Baseball Card Alphabetical Checklist and *Sports Americana Team Baseball Card Checklist* (Sports Americana): Updated editions of these paperbacks are issued every two years. The alphabetical book is a thrill for any collector wanting to specialize in certain players. Instead of reading 900-card lists to find one name, it's possible to find a year-by-year rundown of stars, rookies, or other players.

The team checklist book is just as amazing. Each set's checklist is divided on a team-by-team basis. If you're a fan of, say, the Red Sox, you'll know the exact Boston card numbers from every set.

Team collectors shouldn't be without this book.

Information by Mail

If you want more information about baseball cards, go straight to the source. It's possible to contact card companies by mail if you have questions.

Baseball card companies include:

Classic Games
8055 Troon Circle, Suite C
Austell, GA 30001

Donruss (Leaf)
2355 Waukegan Road
Bannockburn, IL 60015

Fleer
Executive Plaza, Suite 300
1120 Route 73
Mount Laurel, NJ 08054

Pacific Trading Cards
18424 Highway 99
Lynnwood, WA 98037

Score
25 Ford Road
Westport, CT 06880

Topps (Bowman)
254 36th Street
Brooklyn, NY 11232

Upper Deck
5909 Sea Otter Place
Carlsbad, CA 92008

The following is a list of baseball teams. Use these addresses to write to your favorite players, sending them your cards (and a self-addressed, stamped envelope) for autographs. Or write to teams to get promotional schedules, the dates certain teams will give away card sets during designated home games.

Only people attending these games can obtain the cards, but area dealers try to resell the giveaway cards (at a profit, of course) to out-of-town fans later.

AMERICAN LEAGUE

Baltimore Orioles
Oriole Park at Camden Yard
333 West Camden Street
Baltimore, MD 21201

Boston Red Sox
Fenway Park, 4 Yawkey Way
Boston, MA 02215

California Angels
Anaheim Stadium, P.O. Box 2000
Anaheim, CA 92803

Chicago White Sox
333 West 35th Street
Chicago, IL 60616

Cleveland Indians
Cleveland Stadium
Cleveland, OH 44114

Detroit Tigers
Tiger Stadium, 2121 Trumbull Ave.
Detroit, MI 48216

Kansas City Royals
Royals Stadium, P.O. Box 419969
Kansas City, MO 64141

Milwaukee Brewers
County Stadium, 201 S. 46th St.
Milwaukee, WI 53214

Minnesota Twins
H.H.H. Metrodome
501 Chicago Ave. S.
Minneapolis, MN 55415

New York Yankees
Yankee Stadium
Bronx, NY 10451

Oakland Athletics
Oakland-Alameda County Coliseum
Oakland, CA 94621

Seattle Mariners
P.O. Box 4100
Seattle, WA 98104

Texas Rangers
P.O. Box 1111
Arlington, TX 76010

Toronto Blue Jays
Skydome, 300 The Esplanade West
Suite 3200
Toronto, Ontario
Canada M5V 3B3

NATIONAL LEAGUE

Atlanta Braves
Fulton County Stadium
P.O. Box 4064
Atlanta, GA 30312

Chicago Cubs
Wrigley Field
1060 W. Addison St.
Chicago, IL 60613

Cincinnati Reds
Riverfront Stadium
100 Riverfront Stadium
Cincinnati, OH 45202

Colorado Rockies
1700 Broadway, Suite 2100
Denver, CO 80290

Florida Marlins
100 NE Third Ave.
Fort Lauderdale, FL 33301

Houston Astros
The Astrodome, P.O. Box 288
Houston, TX 77001

Los Angeles Dodgers
Dodger Stadium
1000 Elysian Park Ave.
Los Angeles, CA 90012

Montreal Expos
Olympic Stadium
P.O. Box 500, Station "M"
Montreal, Quebec
Canada H1V 3P2

New York Mets
Shea Stadium
126th St. and Roosevelt Ave.
Flushing, NY 11368

Philadelphia Phillies
Veterans Stadium, P.O. Box 7575
Philadelphia, PA 19101

Pittsburgh Pirates
Three Rivers Stadium
P.O. Box 7000
Pittsburgh, PA 15212

St. Louis Cardinals
Busch Stadium
250 Stadium Plaza
St. Louis, MO 63102

San Diego Padres
Jack Murphy Stadium
P.O. Box 2000
San Diego, CA 92120

San Francisco Giants
Candlestick Park
San Francisco, CA 94124

Hall of Fame players can be written to at this address:

c/o National Baseball Hall of Fame
Box 590
Cooperstown, NY 13326

Remember that letters sent across the U.S.-Canadian border require extra postage. And because some teams will move into new stadiums in the coming years, be sure to check for updated addresses at your school or public library. Almanacs and hobby magazines are the best sources for double-checking addresses. Most hobby publications also provide addresses for other teams, manufacturers, and dealers who might offer information or sales lists by mail.

In fact, you might make some pen pals by reading hobby publications. Using the mail is a fast and easy way to keep informed about collecting.

The best collectors never stop improving themselves, or their collections. Keep learning, and you'll find that baseball cards can offer a lifetime of hobby fun.

GLOSSARY

Beckett—the short form of *Beckett Baseball Monthly* magazine or its publisher Dr. James Beckett. Someone who sells at "Beckett" prices uses the magazine's price guide as a guideline.

blankback—a normal card except that all printing was omitted from the back. Although these cards are not common, few people buy or sell them. This limits their value. See also *Wrongback.*

blister pack—a packaging method for card assortments. The cards are surrounded by plastic and attached to a cardboard package, allowing the buyer to see the top card before purchasing.

bonus cards—cards produced not as part of the regular set but to be given away only in packs or rack packs. Occasionally, bonus cards are offered by mail or telephone sales campaigns.

border—the edges, usually white, surrounding the photo area on the front of a card. To be a mint card, all borders must be equal.

Bowman—a card manufacturer that published cards from 1948 to 1955. Originally known as Gum, Inc., Bowman was purchased by Topps, which began issuing sets under the Bowman name in 1989.

box—a vending container issued by card companies to be used by retailers. Usually, 30 to 36 card packs are found in each box.

case—a sealed carton offered by a card company, containing a specified number of factory-collated sets or boxes of card packs.

collectible—(1) an opinion meaning that the card(s) described will be appealing to collectors; (2) a catch-all phrase that includes all non-card items relating to the hobby, such as autographs, team equipment, or baseball books and magazines.

correction—a company's attempt to fix an error card, which corrects a wrong photo, misspelling, or other inaccuracy.

counterfeit—an illegally reprinted version of a card, which has no actual value but is wrongly sold as the actual card.

Diamond Kings—cards issued by Donruss yearly, featuring portraits by artist Dick Perez. Starting with the 1992 edition, these cards were bonus cards (see page 75) and no longer considered part of the regular set.

double-print—a card that is included more than once on a printing sheet from a set.

error—a card containing a mistake in the photo, statistics, or spelling. Cards with errors won't automatically gain in value unless the printer issues corrected versions of the same cards.

factory-collated—the term used to describe complete sets of cards sold in specially designed boxes, sorted in numerical order and sealed by the manufacturer.

foil pack—an individual package of cards, sold by the company in a foil wrapper.

food issue—cards sponsored by a food company as a sales and advertising aid. The cards are sometimes distributed in food packages, or issued in mail or stadium giveaways.

Goudey—a manufacturer of baseball cards from 1933 to 1941.

grade—the term used to describe the physical condition of a baseball card. The grades, from best to worst, are mint, near-mint, excellent, very good, good, fair, and poor.

hand-sorted—the term used to describe complete sets of cards assembled by hand from numerous individual packages. Compare *factory-collated*.

hologram—any of a number of specialized foil-like stickers and cards that give an image or photograph a three-dimensional appearance, created by Upper Deck and other companies.

insert—one specialty item included in individual packages of cards. For instance, Fleer has included a team sticker, while Donruss offers three pieces of a jigsaw puzzle.

memorabilia—non-card items such as autographs, team publications, and equipment. Term similar to *collectible.*

minor-league cards—cards that feature minor-league players. Originally, these cards were printed in individual team sets. Now, large sets containing players from assorted teams are sold in individual packs.

miscut—a card that is removed from the large printing sheet and cut improperly. The card will not have the standard rectangular shape and will have uneven borders.

misprint—a card whose quality was affected by faulty printing, creating a blurry photo, ink blot, streak, or other strange look. Usually, this reduces the value of the card.

National—short for National Sports Collector's Convention. This yearly event is one of the nation's largest card shows, held in a different location each year.

O-Pee-Chee—the Canadian version of Topps cards. O-Pee-Chee cards contain texts in both English and French.

plastic sheet—sheets with pockets for storing cards in a three-ring binder. Plastic sheets hold four to nine cards. See also *sleeve.*

premium—(1) certain limited-edition cards, sometimes autographed, that are inserted into only a few, select packages; (2) the expensive "high end" cards introduced in 1991, sets like Leaf, Fleer Ultra, and Topps Stadium Club.

pre-rookie—the first minor-league cards issued of a player, usually before he's pictured in a major card set as a big leaguer.

preview cards—see *promo cards.*

promo cards—cards circulated by a company before its set appears, in hopes of promoting the upcoming set. Also known as *prototypes* or *preview cards,* promo cards are given as free samples at certain hobby shows or are sent to the media and card dealers to increase publicity and sales.

rack pack—a selection of new cards in a package designed to hang on store racks. Rack packs make it possible for buyers to see beforehand at least one of the cards they'll be buying.

rare—an overused and misunderstood sales term intended to make customers believe the cards being sold are in short supply. See *scarce.*

regional—intended for distribution only in certain geographical regions. Regional card sets may focus on one team and get circulated only in the team's immediate area.

reprint—a later printing of a card, clearly marking the new, nearly identical version of the card as a "reprint." A reprint card also may be re-created in a smaller size or a different card stock, to avoid confusion among collectors.

retro card—cards created years after an actual event, such as a star's playing days in high school or college, and then deceptively sold as rare cards. A variation of counterfeit cards.

rookie card—normally, the first appearance of a new player in a card set.

scarce—a nearly meaningless hobby term used to describe a short supply, similar to "rare."

SCD—*Sports Collectors Digest,* a weekly hobby publication.

sleeve—card-sized plastic pouch used to protect and display cards. See also *plastic sheet.*

Sportflics—a company that issued three-dimensional baseball cards from 1986 to 1990. When tilted at various angles, the plastic-coated cards displayed various images.

starter set—a random number of *different* cards from a certain year of an individual set. A starter set usually excludes most hard-to-get or expensive cards.

team issue—cards printed and distributed directly by a baseball team.

team set—a set comprised of one team's players, separated by a dealer from a major set. A Topps team set of the Dodgers, for example, would include all cards showing members of that team.

traded set—see *update set.*

uncut sheet—an undivided sheet of cards direct from the factory.

update set—set issued since 1981. Update (or traded) sets are released near the season's end, including cards of rookies or traded players in their current team uniforms.

variation—a slightly different version of a card. When a company tries to correct an error card, some new errors may occur. Some variation cards may have one differing color or design element.

wax pack—a pack sold in a waxlike wrapper. Foil or plastic poly-packs have replaced wax.

wrongback—a card that contains the back of another card from that set. A wrongback is more common than a blankback, but neither has a serious chance for increased value.

INDEX